Antarctic Encounter

DESTINATION SOUTH GEORGIA

BY **SALLY PONCET**

PHOTOGRAPHS BY **BEN OSBORNE**

SIMON & SCHUSTER BOOKS FOR YOUNG READERS

Pour Morgane—petite fille dont les cris et les rires
résonnent encore parmi les manchots de Georgie du Sud

ACKNOWLEDGEMENTS
Three people especially helped in the creation of this book. My thanks go to
William Graves for his encouragement and hospitality, to Virginia Duncan at
Four Winds Press and Simon & Schuster for her enthusiasm and, above all, to
Jérôme, who first showed me South Georgia.

The publisher would like to thank the following for permission to reproduce photographs:
Jérôme Poncet: pages 4, 6 *(left)*, 8, 13, 15 *(right top)*; 17, 25 *(left bottom)*, 27 *(top)*, 29 *(above)*, 33
(inset), 38 *(left)*, 41, 48
Peter Prince: 35, 47, *(blue petrel)*, 47 *(dove prion)*
Maps copyright © 1995 by Jeanyee Wong.

SIMON & SCHUSTER BOOKS FOR YOUNG READERS
An imprint of Simon & Schuster Children's Publishing Division
1230 Avenue of the Americas
New York, NY 10020
Text copyright © 1995 by Sally Poncet
Illustrations copyright © 1995 by Ben Osborne
SIMON & SCHUSTER BOOKS FOR YOUNG READERS is a trademark of Simon & Schuster.
Designed by Christy Hale.
The text of this book is set in Bembo.
Manufactured in Hong Kong.
10 9 8 7 6 5 4 3 2 1
Library of Congress Cataloging-in-Publication Data
Poncet, Sally.
Antarctic encounter : destination South Georgia / Sally Poncet :
photographs by Ben Osborne. — 1st ed.
          p.   cm.
1. Natural history—South Georgia Island—Juvenile literature.
2. South Georgia Island—Description and travel—Juvenile
literature. 3. Poncet family—Juvenile literature. [1. South
Georgia Island—Description and travel. 2. Zoology—South Georgia
Island. 3. Zoology—Antarctic regions.] I. Osborne, Ben, ill
II. Title
QH84.2.P65 1995
508.97'11—dc20
94-13376
ISBN 0-02-774905-3

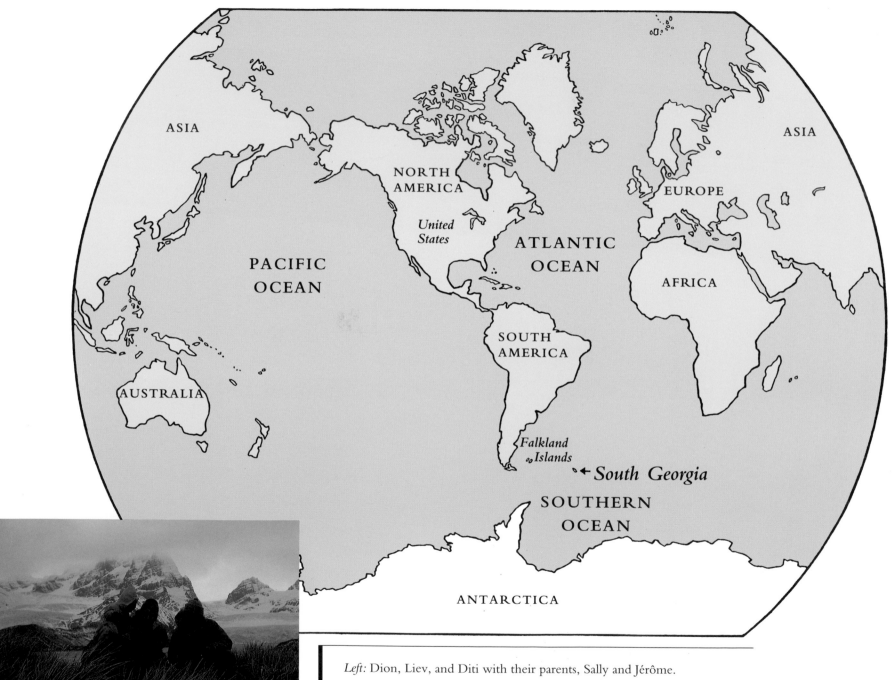

ASIA

NORTH
AMERICA

*United
States*

ATLANTIC
OCEAN

PACIFIC
OCEAN

EUROPE

ASIA

AFRICA

SOUTH
AMERICA

AUSTRALIA

*Falkland
Islands*

← *South Georgia*

SOUTHERN
OCEAN

ANTARCTICA

Left: Dion, Liev, and Diti with their parents, Sally and Jérôme.

Right: Some glaciers in South Georgia descend right down to the sea, ending in a perpendicular wall of ice that towers 50 meters above the boat.

CHAPTER ONE

Most people have a special place that they love above all others. Perhaps yours is a farm you stay at during school holidays or the lake where you go fishing with your best friend; maybe it's the park on the other side of town. Wherever it is, you know it's the right place for you. For the three boys in this story—Dion, eight, Leiv, six, and Diti, three—this special place is an island called South Georgia.

South Georgia: a little speck on the globe, way down near the Antarctic, so far away from any city, road, or airport that you can only get there by boat. Dion, Leiv, and Diti, with their parents, Jérôme and Sally, sail there on their own boat, a small yacht called *Damien II*.

Left: Tucked in a snug little cove, *Damien II* finds shelter from rough seas.

Above: On days of gentle seas, the boys enjoy watching the waves go past and being the first to spot land.

Right: *Damien II*'s lifting keel retracts into a centerboard, leaving a rounded hull that can sit on the beach at low tide. Dion and Leiv go ashore by sliding down a rope.

Damien II is a special yacht, designed for doing exactly what Jérôme and Sally are doing: sailing to the isolated islands of the Southern Ocean and to the ice of the Antarctic. She is built of steel and so is very strong, and because she is also a home, it is warm, cozy, and comfortable inside.

Dion, Leiv, and Diti are used to sailing; *Damien II* has been their home since they were born, and together with Jérôme and Sally they have sailed many miles, all over the world. Of all the places they have seen, South Georgia is their favorite.

Sally and Jérôme are returning to South Georgia to study the seabirds there; to count them and note where they breed. There are few places that can match South Georgia's wildlife: over a million fur seals, three hundred thousand elephant seals, three million macaroni penguins, tens of thousands of albatross and king penguins, and small petrels, in their many millions, all breed here. Only during the summer months, when they lay their eggs and raise their chicks, do the seabirds come in to land. Just how many there are and exactly where they nest is what Jérôme and Sally are trying to find out.

Above: Sally and the boys emerge through the tussock to find themselves on the edge of a huge macaroni penguin colony, where the noise of thousands of penguins calling and fighting is tremendous.

Right top: Sally estimates the number of macaroni nests here, recording the information in her notebook.

When they are not sailing, the family lives in the Falkland Islands, on Beaver Island—a small island whose only other inhabitants are two thousand sheep and quite a few penguins and seals. During the winter months, the children do their school lessons with Sally, and every six weeks there is a two-week visit from a traveling teacher.

During the busy summer months down south, there is no time for traditional school lessons. But the children are learning new skills every day; they chat with scientists about their work, help Jérôme on the boat, and watch Sally take notes about the birds. There are always lots of books to read and plenty of paper and pens for drawing.

Above: Dion tries his hand at sketching an albatross.

Left: Waiting at the airport for the traveling teacher

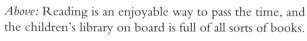

Above: Reading is an enjoyable way to pass the time, and the children's library on board is full of all sorts of books.

Right top: The farm tractor comes in handy for loading stores on board during low tide at Beaver Island.

It's mid-November and summer is just around the corner here in the southern hemisphere. The family set sail five days ago from Stanley in the Falklands, the nearest port to South Georgia. Before leaving, Sally and Jérôme took on board enough food and fuel for the three months' voyage; besides tinned food, there are also fresh vegetables and fruit, eggs, and meat, all of which will keep for weeks, and some for months even, in the cool temperatures of South Georgia.

The wind is whistling and whining its way through the sails and masts. Glistening mountainous seas thunder past, yet down below all is snug and warm. Wedged in with cushions and pillows, the children have fallen asleep with the promise that tomorrow's awakening will bring the end of the ocean: *Damien II* will be in South Georgia.

Above: Wild and somber scenery first greets the visitor to South Georgia: Massive, dark brown mountains patched in snow and ice rise up to pure-white icy summits.

CHAPTER TWO

PALE SHAFTS OF early morning light break through the cloud-darkened horizon. The worst of the night's gale is over, leaving *Damien II* to toss clumsily on the ocean swell, now crosscut by smaller, steeper waves.

Jérôme and Sally have not had much sleep. They took turns looking after *Damien II*, making sure she was on the right course, checking that the sails were set correctly and not chafing, and watching out for icebergs.

Only the children have had a full night's sleep, and as the first light enters the cabin they emerge from their den of

cushions and bedcovers, eager and excited, and asking, "Are we there yet? Can we see the land? How long till we get there?" Diti, unable to wait any longer, climbs up the ladder and is out the hatch and on deck.

The rocky coast is now only a stone's throw away. Patches of kelp, dark brown fronds of swirling seaweed, give warning of land close by. White breakers spurt from the shadows as water meets rock at the foot of the sea cliffs. This is Bird Island, off the northern end of South Georgia. Diti's watching the water ahead: There are fur seals everywhere, swimming in and out of the swirling kelp, diving under and over the waves, and dodging rocks and floating ice.

And, on all sides, from the trough of each wave to the sky above the masts, soar the birds: giant petrels, albatross, prions, storm petrels. A cape pigeon hovers persistently only a few feet from the stern; cormorants—necks outstretched—barely make headway against the breeze; gentoo penguins surface at the bow in a flash of white, orange, and black. Thousands of birds, all here to breed in the summer months.

Dion and Leiv are on deck now, exclaiming excitedly as familiar landmarks appear. Shelter is close. Tucked away behind a zigzag of rocky reefs lies a tiny bay encircled by hills of green tussock. The last point is rounded, and a blue buoy—*Damien II*'s permanent mooring—comes into view. Cries of excitement go up as the children recognize the anchorage, with its small jetty, the green building behind, and the pungent odor of fur seals packed tighter than sardines on the beaches.

"Look, there's Callan and Pete," they cry. Old friends are waiting on the jetty. And the children can't wait to get ashore. There are friendships to renew, and the base buildings and their contents to explore; just to be there is enough. For the children, it's like a homecoming.

Right top: The anchorage at Bird Island provides protection for *Damien II*. The building on the beach is a British base and home for up to 8 scientists who come here to study the birds and seals.

Right: A small stream flowing under the base's walkways provides hours of fun.

CHAPTER THREE

Left: Fur seal puppies, born in early December, take over the base's walkways for the summer.

Below: Bulls, sitting upright, defend their territory against other male intruders; females, back from a feeding trip, stretch out for a rest; and thousands of puppies sleep and play in the tussock and on the beaches.

Right top: Weighing 200 kilograms and capable of moving as fast as a man can run, bull fur seals vigorously defend their territories.

Right middle: Tussock grass grows along most of the coastline of South Georgia, forming a dense canopy 2 meters high in places. It offers an ideal nesting environment for many birds and the stems are also delicious to eat, even if they do tickle your nose.

Right bottom: This black-browed albatross flies many thousands of miles a year.

Far right: This black-browed albatross, sitting on an empty nest, may have lost its egg or chick, or it may have just returned to the colony at the beginning of the breeding season.

"WELCOME BACK!" shouts Pete, a scientist who has been in charge of the base here for over twenty years. "You're just in time for breakfast."

Once *Damien II* is safely secured to her mooring and the rubber dinghy inflated, everyone can go ashore. There are old and new faces to greet; some of the scientists stay over two years on Bird Island; others come just for the summer. With some nervousness, the children follow them through an obstacle course of seals that defend their territory aggressively against intruders. At the moment, the walkways around the base are seal-free but in a month or so they'll be alive with little black bundles of mischief: the adorable fur-seal pups that live under, around, and sometimes inside the base if a door is left open, while their mothers are feeding at sea.

"I don't mind the puppies," says Leiv. "It's those horrible adults I can't stand." A bull, or male, is more than a match for a cautious six-year-old, in speed, weight, and tooth size, and the children have learned to respect these seals as they would a police dog.

After breakfast, Pete invites everyone to accompany him up to his study colony of black-browed albatross. The well-worn track up to the north-facing cliffs on the other side of the island follows a stream through waist-high tussock grass. Although most of the fur seals are crowded together on the beaches for pupping and mating and only move back into the tussock when the pups are older, it is as well to be on the lookout for the odd solitary male: Everyone is equipped with a bodger, which also makes a very good walking stick.

From the top, *Damien II* looks like a toy boat on a pond. Albatross glide past, riding the air currents above the tussock slopes. The children enjoy watching them, feeling the whoosh and brush of air as the big white-and-black birds pass only a few feet above their heads.

At the colony on the cliffs the black-brows are on their nests, each incubating a single white egg. Pete loves it up here, sitting quietly and watching the birds. He has banded every individual in this particular colony by fitting a numbered plastic ring around its leg. This means that from one year to the next he can follow the life of each bird when it returns to breed.

Pete also weighs the chicks just before they are fed by their parents, and just after, so that he can find out how much food they eat. At first, he had to do this by sitting for hours, waiting for the birds to come in, ready to run to the chick, place it on the scales, put it back on the nest, and then reweigh it. Not surprisingly, Pete decided that there had to be an easier way to do it. He developed what he calls "automatic nests"; once a bird has laid her egg, Pete replaces the real nest with a plastic one and puts the bird and her egg in it. Underneath each plastic nest is an electronic balance that automatically weighs the chick. This information is sent through wires to a computer in a nearby hut. Pete visits the hut daily to check that the instruments are working correctly.

Left: An albatross chick hatches in December and is fed krill and fish by its parents until it is ready to fledge in April. The young bird spends the next 3 to 5 years circling the oceans before returning to South Georgia.

Below and right: Before the age of electronics, scientists had to measure, weigh, and record by hand. Here a chick is placed on the scales and its weight recorded in a notebook. Today, plastic nests with automatic weight sensors make the scientist's job much easier; all the information is sent through wires from the nest to a computer.

CHAPTER FOUR

"BUT WE DON'T WANT TO GO," protests a small voice, as Sally and Jérôme debate whether to leave Bird Island. The wind is still blowing hard; mist pours over the hills above the anchorage, and the rocks at the entrance are fringed with white breakers.

"We'll be back here for Christmas, Leiv. And besides, we're on our way to Leith Harbour, then Grytviken." The magic of South Georgia's deserted whaling stations is waiting; memories of past summers' explorations, the treasures found, the secret places, are still strong. Leiv's smile returns.

"Ready to cast off?" Jérôme shouts as Sally prepares to untie the mooring rope. Strong gusts push *Damien II* from the sheltered waters of the anchorage out into the massive swell in Bird Sound. The boat twists this way and that from trough to crest as seas break on all sides, flooding the deck in whirlpools of water.

Dion, Leiv, and Diti, after waving good-bye, have returned to the safety and comfort of their bunks. Here, the roller-coaster sensations and stomach-churning movement are almost enjoyable, despite the jarring, shuddering vibrations of the hull as it hits a wave and the clatter and crash of a stray cup that rolls across the floor. Sally is busy making sure that nothing else is about to fall and reassuring Diti that it will get calmer very soon and that he will then be able to eat his breakfast.

Once Bird Sound is well astern, the movement becomes less violent. Outside, there is sunlight on the water ahead, and Bird Island disappears.

The course is set for Right Whale Bay, fifteen nautical miles to the east, and as the wind dies down and the seas become calmer, sailing becomes sheer pleasure. The gusty southwest wind that funneled into Bird Sound is now a regular breeze and *Damien II*, under self-steering, all sails set, glides smoothly over the water at seven knots. Down below, Diti is having breakfast while Sally unfolds maps and sorts through her notes from previous seasons. Dion and Leiv are back to their favorite pastime, drawing.

Out on deck, Jérôme keeps an eye on the boat's position. Although it is not necessary to stand at the wheel when the boat's self-steering is on, it is important to know exactly where you are at all times when close inshore; some areas of South Georgia have not been thoroughly explored, and there are uncharted rocks in unexpected places. So Jérôme always follows the depth sounder, mounted outside in the cockpit, and looks out for kelp patches and disturbed water that could indicate shallow water or reefs.

Left: Rough seas and strong winds can be exciting on a small boat, as the bow hits the waves and water comes pouring over the deck.

Below: A yacht the size of *Damien II* only needs one person to sail her. Sally and Jérôme take turns in keeping watch on deck and adjusting the sails.

As Cape North is rounded, everyone is on deck. Jérôme has brought the boat close to the shore, and on the cliffs above, among the tussock, are colonies of black-browed and grey-headed albatross.

The boat is only twenty meters from the cliffs, and there's no need to use binoculars to see the birds here! Being this close in means that you can see exactly what species of birds are nesting, what the terrain is like, and even what types of plants are growing. All of these details are noted by Sally on her maps.

Above: Grey-headed albatross nest on steep tussock slopes, arriving back at the colony in September, a month earlier than the black-brows.

20

Below: Once killed for their beautiful sleek fur, the fur seals in South Georgia are now protected. The total population is estimated at 2 million animals and is still increasing.

As the boat follows the coast southeast from Cape North around to Nameless Point and then doubles back southwest into the shelter of the bay, the cliffs give way to hills and vales of tussock rising to steep scree slopes behind. Sally scans the area. Here and there are a few white dots: wandering albatross on their nests. Through binoculars, Sally can see giant petrels. From the beaches come the noise and smell of fur seal, much to Leiv's disgust.

"Don't say they're here, too!" he complains. Fur seals effectively render some beaches out-of-bounds to children, and most adults. Although the seals are not as numerous here as they are on Bird Island, their numbers have definitely increased since Jérôme and Sally's visit two years ago. This is good news for the seals, which are at last recovering from virtual extinction, caused by sealers in the last century, but it's not so good for the birds in areas where the seals are disturbing them on their nests.

The anchor chain rattles to rest on the sand and mud in Right Whale Bay. The sun sparkles on the calm water as it does on the snow fields above; the dark sand on the beach shimmers in heat waves. It's a beautiful afternoon of blue skies and crisp air.

Left: There are now 40 colonies of kings in South Georgia, and this one at Right Whale Bay has 7,000 pairs.

CHAPTER FIVE

COME ON, LET'S GO!" THE children shout, ever eager to get ashore and stretch their legs. Leiv, equipped with a rucksack packed with toy boats and trucks, is first in the dinghy, quickly followed by Dion, who has the outboard running while everyone else clambers in. Choosing a landing site is a tricky business when fur seals are about; avoiding the densely packed sand, the dinghy heads for the rocky shore at the edge of the beach.

Sally and Jérôme have work to do near the landing beach, and while they are counting the nests in the several gentoo colonies here, the children play happily among the rock pools with their toys, well away from the seals.

There is a big king penguin colony close behind the beach, and from it comes a continuous background noise of musical trumpeting from the adult birds, accompanied by a soft whistling from the chicks. Kings are the most beautiful

23

of all penguins; the adults have two brilliant, deep orange "ear" patches that extend to a golden breast, fading to a soft, shiny white front, all contrasting magnificently with the steel-gray back.

The penguins move quietly within the colony. Even when confronted with such unpredictable creatures as humans, they retain their regal bearing. A small group marches in single file past Diti, who is sitting on the beach, too engrossed with his trucks to notice them. Nearly one meter tall, they tower over Diti, who only looks up when a fluffy brown chick, almost as tall as its parents, wanders up to inspect him from a short distance. Like a shapeless brown beanbag, the down-covered chick plumps itself at Diti's feet and watches curiously, leaning forward with its beak as

Far left: An early morning swim in the surf is part of the daily routine for adult king penguins during their time ashore in an often muddy colony. After a short bath, the birds return to their chicks, plumage sparkling clean.

Left: Nearly fully grown, these fluffy brown king penguin chicks band together in crèches.

Below: A group of king penguins walks sedately past Diti.

Right: The magnificent adult king penguin in full breeding plumage.

if to inspect this strange creature. Other chicks join it, too. Some of them are near to fledgling; their down is being replaced here and there by adult black-and-white plumage, and the children can't help laughing at their appearance—the smartness of their sleek new feathers ruined by a mop of unruly down on the head.

"Come look!" says Diti. "I've found a little tunnel."

"That's a rat hole," says Dion, "and there are some droppings."

"I saw a rat at Leith Harbour once," adds Leiv.

"Well, that explains why there are no birds there or here," says Sally, who has just returned with Jérôme. "No pipits, no prions, and no burrows, except for these rat holes. The rats have killed all the birds little by little."

Rats probably arrived in South Georgia with the first sealers, two hundred years ago. They came ashore in the ships' stores, even swam ashore if a ship was wrecked, as often happened. And when the whaling stations were built at the beginning of this century, the rats found plenty of food and shelter in the buildings. But they can also survive on tussock grass and so have spread all along the coast, eating birds, chicks, and eggs as they go. Only water and glaciers can stop the rats from spreading. And wherever they have gone, the small birds and petrels have disappeared.

"Come and see us race our boats," Dion and Leiv continue. "There's a really good stream over there, past those weanies." This season's elephant seal pups, now weaned, doze like gray slugs here and there on the beach. Weanies are sweet, say the children. They don't mind being tickled gently, nor do they wake up in a bad temper like fur seals do as you walk past. And if they do see you, they usually go back to sleep anyway, if you don't disturb them. So, the children, mindful of the weanies, continue their races, splashing in and out of the water, oblivious to wet hands and water-filled boots.

"I wish it was hot enough to go swimming," says Dion, remembering another sunny afternoon two years ago, when they'd picnicked on the beach and he'd gone swimming in a pool beneath a waterfall. Today, there's a slight breeze that sharpens the chill of near-zero temperatures and carries away the warmth of the sun.

"Time to go back to the boat," says Sally, before cold feet and hands spoil the afternoon.

Top: Elephant seal pups, born in October, have 27 days in which to grow fat and sleek before their mother weans them.

Above: Some days, the weather surprises everyone; Dion joins the weanies for a dip beneath a waterfall.

CHAPTER SIX

Above: The kitchen counter is a favorite spot for Diti.

HOW NICE IT IS TO RETURN to the warmth of the boat, to hang wet socks and trousers above the stove to dry, and to snuggle up on the sheepskin rugs while sipping a hot drink. Diti falls asleep, and Jérôme does, too, still tired from the previous nights' watches.

Dion and Leiv, though, get back to boats, this time making them out of Legos, with preliminary trials in the kitchen sink. There's not a lot of room in the kitchen, or galley, as it's called on a boat, and when Sally asks for help making bread, the toys are put away. Dion measures out cupfuls of flour into a big basin while Sally adds the salt, yeast, and oil, and Leiv pours in warm water. These are all mixed together into a soft, stretchy dough and left to rise in the warm spot behind the stove. Then the dough is ready to make into bread, of any shape you like, and Dion and Leiv have fun plaiting it into loaves and shaping rolls into fish and men with raisin eyes.

While the dough is rising, Sally writes up her day's observations; as well as counting birds, she does sketch maps of the coast, marking in the bird colonies, seal beaches, tussock grass, and also kelp patches, rocks, and depth of water offshore—reminders for future navigations. There are cards to fill in—a checklist of the birds seen in a certain area. All this data will be used to find out just where the birds are breeding and how many there are in South Georgia. It may take two years or more to complete the survey, and just as long again to analyze the information.

Above: Snow can fall in any month of the year in South Georgia but rarely lasts for long at sea level during the summer. The snowman on deck, looking suspiciously like Jérôme, will melt by lunchtime.

Right: Here is one of Sally's survey charts, which is coded to indicate evidence of possible, probable or confirmed breeding of different bird species in an area. For example, "NE" means that nests with eggs have been discovered, and "NY" means that nests with young are present, both signs of confirmed breeding. Columns one and two indicate more uncertainty; for example, "N" means the bird has been spotted visiting a probable nest site, but further clues have not been found.

landings

SOUTH GEORGIA BREEDING BIRD SURVEY CAPE NORTH AREA					RATS		
GRID SQUARE (D.O.S. MAP) A 8				**DATE** 20.1.87			
OBSERVER(S) S. Poncet	1	2	3		1	2	3
KING PENGUIN				FAIRY PRION			
CHINSTRAP PENGUIN				WHITE-CHINNED PETREL			UN
GENTOO PENGUIN			NY	WILSONS STORM PETREL	✓		
MACARONI PENGUIN			NE	BLACK-BELLIED STORM PETREL			
ROCKHOPPER PENGUIN				GREY-BACKED STORM PETREL			
WANDERING ALBATROSS				SOUTH GEORGIA DIVING PETREL			
BLACK-BROWED ALBATROSS			NY	COMMON DIVING PETREL			
GREY-HEADED ALBATROSS			ON	BLUE EYED SHAG			NY
LIGHT-MANTLED SOOTY ALBATROSS			NY	BROWN SKUA			ON
SOUTHERN GIANT PETREL			NY	DOMINICAN GULL			ON
NORTHERN GIANT PETREL		N		ANTARCTIC TERN			ON
CAPE PIGEON				SOUTH GEORGIA PINTAIL	✓		
SNOW PETREL				SPECKLED TEAL			
BLUE PETREL				SHEATHBILL			ON
DOVE PRION				SOUTH GEORGIA PIPIT			

Right: From Albatross Island in the Bay of Isles, there is a splendid view of the mainland of South Georgia.

THE NEXT DAY STARTS OFF miserably. Low clouds blanket the coast, snowflakes flutter lightly to the deck, and it looks like the wind is getting up. The anchor chain grumbles with each gust, and the boat tugs impatiently, as if wanting to go. Dion and Leiv want to go, too; for each mile will bring them closer to Leith Harbour. "Will we get there tonight?" they ask hopefully.

"In two days' time, we'll be there," declares Jérôme, "after we've visited the Bay of Isles. So clear up the toys and books; it could be bumpy outside."

It is bumpy, but fortunately, it's only a short hop down the coast, and once they're underway, the wind disappears.

The Bay of Isles is in sunshine, and although the mountaintops are covered in cloud, the enormous glaciers that descend from the summits are glowing with light. Out in the bay, the dozen or so islands and rocks that give the bay its name are a lush green contrast. Most of the islands are named after birds—Prion, Petrel, Skua, Tern, Mollyhawk, and Albatross—and with good reason: They are wonderful places for birds.

The nearest islands are less than half a mile away, and Jérôme asks Dion to take the wheel while he goes below to warm up with a quick cup of coffee. "Keep an eye out for kelp," he warns.

Dion's quite happy to be in charge, with Sally close by, busily sketching the islands and wanting to know how deep it is. "Over thirty meters," Dion says, skirting around the edge of a big kelp patch, "but decreasing now." He eases back the throttle as Jérôme returns to take the wheel, bringing the boat into the channel between Mollyhawk and Invisible islands.

"Still fifteen meters, but we'll have to anchor here," Jérôme announces. "That looks like a rock ahead."

"Do you think there are any fur seals here?" asks Leiv. "That tussock over there looks all flattened—there could be some hiding there." Equipped with bodgers, everyone goes ashore. Jérôme leads the way through the tussock, which, to Leiv's relief, is only inhabited by giant petrels today. These large seabirds are sitting on their nests of tussock grass strands.

"Don't go too close, Diti," warns Sally. "Some of them are very shy and might fly away."

"Or they'll squirt that smelly red liquid all over you," says Dion.

The sealers called these birds "stinkers" or "nellies." They are not as beautiful as the albatross, and the sealers didn't like them very much, because of their habit of gorging themselves on dead and dying animals. They eat so much and become so heavy that, in order to take off, they have to vomit up their meals. The sealers didn't think much of that, either.

Mollyhawk is a typical tussock island, covered in waist-high grass from the beach to the upper slopes. Pushing through it is hard work for children: The long leaves brush their faces and tickle their noses, and underfoot it can be slippery and muddy. Diti's fallen over again, but has spotted a burrow while down beneath the tussock.

"Rats?" he asks.

"I hope not," says Jérôme. "Let's have a look down inside."

Above: By tearing an opening in the skin through which it pokes its entire head, a giant petrel feasts on the bloodied flesh and intestines of a newborn elephant seal pup. A skua stands close by, ready to take over when the giant petrel can eat no more.

Inset: The only way these birds can take off if disturbed after a full meal is to vomit the contents of their stomachs: in this case a mixture of intestines and two partially disgested eyeballs.

Left: Arriving from the sea in huge flocks, dove prions usually come and go from their burrows under the cover of darkness.

Above: There are millions of dove prions breeding in South Georgia. In some areas, the ground beneath the tussock is so riddled with their burrows that you cannot walk without breaking through the surface.

Lying outstreched on the ground, he carefully puts his hand down the burrow, further and further and further, until only his shoulder is showing. "It's a deep one. Ouch! And there's someone at home." Jérôme gently takes the soft, warm body in his fingers, trying to avoid the sharp bill, and brings it to the surface. The children are still wondering if it's a rat. "Blue petrel or dove prion?" he asks Sally as the bird emerges into daylight. The small bird, held firmly in Jérôme's hand, is a soft, smoky blue-gray color, with a darker *M* pattern across its wings. It's a dove prion, one of the most common birds breeding in South Georgia—where there are no rats. A low cooing noise comes from below the ground as other prions call from their burrows. Carefully, Jérôme returns the bird to its nest.

Further up the slope, Leiv is startled by a small brown shape flashing past in a whirr of feathers. "Hey, a duck!" he says. "It almost flew into me."

"I bet the bird got a fright, too," says Sally. "She was probably sitting on her nest. Did you see exactly where she flew out from?"

"Yes, just here. Oh, look! Here it is: four eggs and a beautiful nest."

Left top: With a wingspan of over 3 meters, the wandering albatross is the largest of all seabirds.

Above: Life is tough for a young wanderer chick, waiting patiently through winter storms and heavy snowfalls for its parents to return.

Left bottom: The chicks hatch at the end of summer and are fed all through the winter months by parents that may fly as far as Brazil looking for food.

It's not far to the top now, and the tussock gives way to small areas of short, fine grass and moss, just like a meadow. The top of the island is quite flat, and dotted not with white woolly sheep but beautiful snow-white birds: the wandering albatross.

"Will they peck me?" asks Diti anxiously.

Dion replies, teasing, "Yes, and they'll eat you up, too!"

Certainly they must look huge to Diti: taller than he is, they snap their bills noisily if you come too close. But Diti's not about to get any closer. There are three pairs here, all too busy with their courtship dances to take much notice of the passersby. With wings outstretched, two birds face each other, bow gracefully, and make a loud bill-clappering noise, before throwing their heads back to finish with a braying whistle.

It's a beautiful spot to sit and watch them. Pipits, small songbirds with a soft piping call, twitter from the tussock. A yellow-billed pintail flies overhead; its plaintive cricket-like whistle unexpectedly reminds you of a warm tropical evening rather than a cool morning in South Georgia.

"I could lie here for hours," says Sally.

"Well, not me," says Dion. "How far is it to Leith Harbour now?"

Above: Adult wandering albatross pair for life, reinforcing their bond with this lovely courtship dance in early summer before settling down to egg laying.

CHAPTER EIGHT

AT LONG LAST THE RUSTY RED rooftops of Leith Harbour appear at the head of Stromness Bay. The whaling station is a tiny jumble of boxes at the foot of the mountains. As the yacht sails up to the shelter of the little port tucked away behind the last point, the children are on deck, pointing out their favorite buildings, the football field, the stream. The lines aren't even secured and the children have jumped ashore; their playground, a maze of empty buildings, contents scattered from attic to ground floor and out into the lanes, awaits them, as fresh in their minds as the day they left it, almost a year ago.

Above and left: Over 175,000 whales were taken at South Georgia between 1904 and 1965. Many were processed here at the Leith Harbour whaling station.

Far left: Despite the huge numbers of whales killed, there are still some left today. When their paths cross with *Damien II,* both whales and family stop to say hello.

"Sally, come and see! Our bath's still here, and my toys."

Leiv is overjoyed at the sight. These "toys"—cogs, wheels, pipes, and axles—are beautiful wooden replicas of the cast iron machinery parts that were forged in the blacksmith's shop at Leith.

"Look, here's the forge, and that's where the wooden toys come from, up there." Past crumbling jetties, through winding passages, they emerge at the water's edge.

Above and right: The boys can splash as much as they like during bathtime in the little shed on the port, while outside the snow falls in heavy white flakes.

40

The large wooden platform, a giant chopping board for carving up whales, lies silent, surrounded by sheds and rusty machinery. Rickety stairways lead to upper storeys, and wobbly handrails, missing floorboards, and long overhead catwalks all add up to one gigantic playground where the children play hide-and-seek. There are dark cupboards to investigate, doorways leading to secret rooms, the musty odors of dried whale meat, rats, old books, and moldy rags. Among all this, there are countless treasures that the children are always bringing back to the boat: strange pieces of metal, little wooden boxes, bottles, bits of baleen and whale bone, fire extinguishers, shiny taps, a saucepan.

"Is there time to go to the hospital?" they ask. Walking past the laboratory, they look in through the open door.

"Careful, there's broken glass everywhere, Diti."

Though the laboratory was once clean and orderly, uncaring visitors have smashed the shiny glass funnels, test tubes, and bottles. Windows stare back, empty and silent.

"Let's go back, it's getting dark."

Top: Touring Leith Harbour in style: An old hand cart becomes a carriage.

Middle: Formerly, huge pieces of whale meat were winched up this ramp to the meat loft above. This gigantic slide now lies rusting, used only by Dion and Leiv.

Bottom: The first whaling station and permanent settlement in South Georgia was established here at Grytviken in 1904.

The derelict buildings, as the evening light fades, are so lonely. Broken windows, swinging, creaking doors, loose sheets of roofing iron tapping in the wind, water pouring from a burst pipe. All is abandoned and wrecked, where once a thousand men worked day and night, killing the whales.

There'll be time tomorrow morning to visit the hospital, and sit in the dentist's chair again; to climb to the attic and look out the tiny window over the bay. "And don't forget, there's the dam to see, and the fort on the hill."

"Could we have a bath tomorrow? We don't have to go, do we?"

Jérôme assures the boys that there will be plenty of time tomorrow and that they'll be back several more times, too.

"I wish I could live here, in my own house." Dion sighs.

"I'd get the generators going, clean up the rubbish, fix the windows. I'd make it into a real town again, with a shop at the post office, and once a week we'd show a film at the old cinema."

"And I'd fix up that wooden dinghy in the guano shed," continues Leiv. "And go fishing. We could smoke the fish with those bundles of twigs on the jetty, just like the whalers used to."

"And in winter we'd get the ski tow running and go ice-skating on the lake behind the dam."

Above: The whale catcher *Petrel,* with a harpoon cannon mounted on the bow, worked out of Grytviken before World War II. The explosive harpoon was 2 meters long, and after a high-speed chase was fired into the whale at very short range.

Dion and Leiv make their plans for the future, dreaming of a make-believe world that might, one day, exist. For the moment, South Georgia remains isolated, and its birds and animals live there in peace. Jérôme and Sally hope it remains that way. They leave the future to Dion, Leiv, and Diti, who will dream of South Georgia for many years to come, forever wishing to return.

Willis Islands

Bird Island *Bird Sound*

Cape North

Nameless Point ↓
Right Whale Bay

Mollyhawk Island ↓
Albatross Island ↓
Invisible Island

Bay of Isles

Prince Olav Harbour

Leith Harbour
Stromness Bay

Stromness ●
Husvik ●

Grytviken ●

0   10   20   KILOMETERS
0 5   10   15   MILES

South Georgia

SOUTHERN
OCEAN

N
W   E
S

SOME ANIMAL SPECIES FOUND IN SOUTH GEORGIA

Black-browed albatross
Black-browed albatross start breeding when they are seven years old and may live for another thirty years.

←

Grey-headed albatross
A pair of grey-headed albatross reinforce their bond by nibbling and preening each other.

←

Wandering albatross
A wandering albatross may fly from South Georgia to Brazil and back looking for squid to feed its chick. ➡

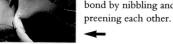

Blue-eyed cormorant
Blue-eyed cormorants breed in small colonies that are scattered all along the coast of South Georgia.

←

Pintail ➡
Pintails usually feed in freshwater ponds but on occasion will help themselves to the flesh of dead fur seals.

Gentoo penguin
About one-third of the world's gentoo penguins breed on South Georgia. ←

King penguin
A king penguin chick is fed by its parents for about a year before it is ready to leave the colony for the ocean. →

Macaroni penguin
Macaroni penguins still have scientists puzzled about why the penguins usually discard the first of their two eggs. ←

Blue petrel
Blue petrels lay a single egg underground in a snug nest chamber, which is at the end of a burrow that can be up to two meters (over six and a half feet) long. ↑

Giant petrel
Giant petrels are the carrion feeders of the Antarctic, eating any dead or dying animal. →

Wilson's storm petrel
Wilson's storm petrels are one of the smallest and most numerous seabirds in the world. ←

Cape pigeon
Cape pigeons often follow ships, ever on the lookout for scraps of food. →

Pipit
The South Georgia pipit, although closely related to pipits in the Falklands and South America, is a distinct species found only in South Georgia in areas where there are no rats. ←

Dove prion
Dove prions also lay their single egg underground, and in some places the soil beneath the tussock grass is honeycombed with their burrows.

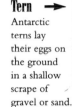

Fur seal
Fur seals crowd South Georgia's beaches in December and January. ←

Elephant seal →

Elephant seals are in their element under water, diving down to 1500 meters (over 4900 feet) to catch squid and fish.

Brown skua →
Brown skuas keep a keen lookout for intruders to their territory, ever ready to defend their nests and chicks by aggressive aerial dive-bombings.

Tern →
Antarctic terns lay their eggs on the ground in a shallow scrape of gravel or sand.

Cape Disappointment